Against All Odds
The Story of a Norfolk Garden

The cottage and its garden.

Against All Odds

The Story of a Norfolk Garden

Barbara Sommerville

Marius Press

11 Kirklands Road, Over Kellet, Carnforth,
Lancashire LA6 1DP, UK

A CIP catalogue record is available from the British Library.

ISBN: 978-1-871622-98-0

Designed by the Drawing Room Design, Over Kellet, UK
Printed and bound in the UK

Contents

Illustrations

Preface

A garden is a joysome thing! Anonymous, I think, and so it should be, because the joy is seriously tempered by a multitude of unjoyful things like weather, weeds and wigglies – but more of these anon.

This is a light-hearted account of how I set out to find a piece of land in the country in which I could create a garden. As it turned out, the piece of land that I was eventually lucky enough to find proved to have everything about it that a gardener would wish to avoid – fine sand, drought, alkalinity and an abundance of rabbits, voles, moles and deer. The story charts how my obdurate personality, bit by bit, overcame all these obstacles and created a beautiful garden. It deals a little with the Norfolk background and history, as well as with the characters who helped me dig and build, and quite a lot with the coping engineering I developed by trial and error. It has a wealth of gardening know-how for anyone struggling with such problems, as well as some history of life in what is now Norfolk.

Barbara Sommerville
Oxborough, 2016

Acknowledgements

I should like to thank cordially all my friends who have given me so much help and encouragement, some in a professional capacity and some just imposed upon: Mervyn May, Bob Bennet, Peter Hurrell, Rocky Easter, Roger Keay, Jan and Stewart Waterston and Bar and Geoff Pritchard.

Last but not least I should like to thank my daughter Sophie for efficient fencing and more, Neil and Susan Johnson who have acted as conscientious editors and publishers, and an old friend Anne Turnbull who put me in touch with them.

For the old photos I am indebted to Kelvin Smith and the postcards from the John Stocking collection as well as the Norfolk Museums Service and the Suffolk Museums Service. I must also mention my gratitude for all the "warrening" information which I got from the Breckland Society Report *The Warrens of Breckland: A Survey by the Breckland Society*, co-written by Anne Mason and James Parry and edited by Liz Dittner.

The photo of me which appears on the back cover was taken by my old friend Jo Banks.

Landmark features of the garden

B	*The large box*
C	*Cercis "Forest Pansy"*
D	*The dew pond*
G	*One of the gravel beds*
H	*The rabbit Ha-ha*
S	*The early sunken bed*
W	*Wild-flower area within the Ha-ha.*

The grassy walk between the old oak tree and the larch. The newel post was placed near the oak on the sight-line between the two trees.

L *The big larch*

O *The old oak*

A lily in the pale

1

In the Beginning

To me, a garden is one of life's essentials. Human beings need nature. They need space to escape the pettiness of everyday demands and feel their primeval roots in damp earth. They need to commune with plants; to cherish the crusty texture of an oak tree trunk and gaze up in wonderment at its massive size and age; to admire the beauty of a young ivy frond and the ethereal elegance of a lily. They need somewhere to get despicably muddy – a huge release for pent up inhibitions.

My mother gave me a tiny bit of our garden for my own when I was about six. I guess I must have been asking for this. In the spring an older cousin helped me buy flower seeds and plant them. I can still vividly recall those flowers I grew: there were delicately scented mignonette, godetia, eschscholzia, Canterbury bells and candytuft. I was immensely proud of my first flowers.

The place in which I really became an adult gardener was Yorkshire, where I had quite a large garden and devoted every spare minute to it – not that I had many of these, what with running a part-time job, bringing up a load of kids and supporting local activities in the peace movement.

Then I decided this was a crazy way to spend one's life. Gardens are ephemeral; neglect them for one season and there is not much surviving except trees and "weeds." I got a new full-time job and moved to an inner-city terrace.

It was a nice end-terrace, but badly in need of TLC. There were four steep steps leading from a pedestrian precinct up to the front door. I had brought with me from Yorkshire two "Peggy" tubs which were used to wash the clothes in before the advent of washing machines. These I rust treated, painted the original dull silver and placed beside the steps. I planted them with wisteria, jasmine and bedding plants.

My only other gardening area was a back yard at basement level which measured fourteen feet by eight and was paved. So I installed two millstone-grit troughs, also originating in Yorkshire. The men who delivered all my effects when I moved in seemed less than enthusiastic about my troughs. It probably had something to do with the necessity of carrying them up the front steps, through the living room and then down a flight of steps to the back door and yard. Planted up with alpines they graced the yard well and I managed to increase the effective size of this by building a veranda which could be reached through French windows from the kitchen, with a small spiral staircase leading down into the yard.

1. The veranda in the back yard of my city terrace.

Beneath the veranda were stowed bikes and all the potentially useful things I couldn't bear to throw away, while on top I had a small sitting area. There was already a very floriferous red rambler rose growing up behind the veranda and I added a vigorous pale apricot rose, Lady Hillingdon, by the French windows. It swarmed up the wall fast, reaching higher than my bedroom window, and bore lovely elongated blooms which drooped so one could stand on the veranda and admire them. It flowered from May until November and the new foliage was an attractive bronze.

After three years, my tiny back yard seemed to lack further challenge and, with retirement looming, I began to venture out each weekend to search for a place in the country. I ignored my previous conviction that devoting one's self to a large garden was not a sensible life commitment. Looking back I don't think I had really convinced myself about this at all. I have always found it difficult to curtail my activities on the grounds of "sensible" advice – even my own. I decided that this place in the country should be at least one acre in area and have on it a supply of water and electricity, essential for serious gardening. I also reasoned that my bank balance would just stretch to a derelict cottage maybe, but it would have to be in Norfolk and away from the coast to be accessible for weekend commuting and affordable.

Each Saturday throughout September I jubilantly loaded my bike into the back of the car and set off for all the small towns in the chosen area. I was armed with a deck of paper slips stating my needs, and I presented one to each estate agent I could find. They read it politely and then smiled apologetically, or even laughed outright, and said "You'll be lucky. Not seen anything like that for the last fifteen years – *and* there are a lot of people out there looking for it!" Being an eternal optimist, I then cycled around to investigate any bit of land that appeared to be abandoned.

Come October I loaded my bike with a determined set to my jaw and decided to cycle round poking about a bit more. It was beginning to dawn on me that Norfolk was largely owned by a few pretty rich people who were unlikely to sell off an acre of their vast estates to someone like me. The derelict cottages seemed thin on the ground, too.

By November it was with a dogged air that I loaded my bike each Saturday. I was becoming familiar with the time-warp of quaint run-down little villages where I chatted to some elderly folk tending their spacious cottage gardens. They patiently explained that the local squire owned not only this village but all the nearby villages and the surrounding countryside as well. By contrast, there were a few boom villages in multiple private ownership – immaculately neat, with bottle-bottom glass mini-bay-windows – and with miniscule gardens because two new bungalows had been squeezed in beside them. When I posed leading questions about land for sale there, I would be told the exorbitant price being asked for a tiny parcel with planning permission for three more bungalows.

The last Saturday of November the bike was loaded with desperation, but I planned to present my slips of paper to the estate agents for one last time – just in case a miracle happened. Just before 5 p.m. I had delivered them to the last town, and I enquired whether there were any more agents that I might have missed. I was told that at the far end of the market place was *Just Bungalows*. I cringed. Norfolk is a haven for small and large estates of concrete-block and brick boxes called bungalows, but I had one slip left and I do like to finish a job, so off I went.

Just Bungalows seemed slightly more sympathetic than usual and the smile was gentler: “You'll be lucky. It must be about fifteen years since we had anything like that – *and* there are a lot of people out there looking for it!” I drove sadly home, thinking I should give it a break until the spring when I might hit upon a different strategy.

Wednesday morning brought a *Just Bungalows* envelope which I opened unenthusiastically. To my amazement there was a photo of a late Georgian pale-brick bungalow with a very low-pitched four-square-hipped roof, chimney issuing from the centre. It was clearly in a poor state because they asked for offers below my top price and there was not only nearly one acre of land round it but another one-and-a-half acres a quarter of a mile away beside the river for an extra £5,000. Behind the bungalow was a towering old oak tree, and a bit of the front door peeped out through colossal box bushes. I immediately telephoned for an appointment to view the following Saturday.

2. The bungalow in the *Just Bungalows* sales brochure.

The cottage sat on a little knoll. The land surrounding it was full of a suckering plum crossed with a wild one, and lilac so venerable that many of the ten-inch-diameter trunks were horizontal: any space between these was packed with nettles.

3. The garden as it was.

It was a mile up a mainly unmade track full of potholes, and as I peered through the trees only the empty cottage next door was visible and no other habitation or even a telegraph pole in sight. *Bliss!*

Fearful of being "gazumped" I offered their asking price and summoned a surveyor and an electrician. The septic tank seemed OK but the borehole pump needed replacing, and the cheap metal light-fitting hanging from the centre of the sitting room ceiling registered 250 volts: the electrician marched straight to the meter cupboard and turned off the supply. Still, I did, potentially at least, have electricity and water, and I successfully reduced my cottage offer to include the wood and riverside land.

4. The land surrounding the cottage was full of a suckering plum crossed with a wild one

Originally, the cottage had had two small sash-windows on each side. Unfortunately the previous owners had been enthusiastic DIY "improvers" and had replaced all but three windows with massive metal framed orifices. Happily, the three remaining windows had their original draw down/up wooden shutters and I would have to replace the vandalised ones with double-glazed modern windows of the same proportions and apparent pane size as the old ones. The previous owners had built onto the back of the bungalow a flat-roofed extension which had been abandoned in an unfinished state and rain poured in through its roof. The floor was covered with overflowing buckets and cans. I was going to need a substantial mortgage to put all this to rights.

5. Not a telegraph pole in sight. *Bliss!*

2

A Place in the Country

Full of elation, I arranged the mortgage and contacted local builders. The mortgage was reasonably easy, but the builders seemed reluctant. I asked local advice, but all I got, unhelpfully, was "If he's got time to do the job don't touch him." I selected one of them and later, after getting horrendously close to a court case when I refused to pay any more escalating costs, lived to regret it.

Instead of in spring, as arranged, the rebuilding began in midsummer and each month I received an unitemized bill. By October a new raised roof covering the entire cottage and extension was in place, but the front was not slated and the new bathroom and porch were unbuilt. I had by then paid more than the original estimate to complete the job, so I refused to pay the last instalment until I had all the work to date priced. With dire threats of taking me to court, the builder stopped work. This, of course, risked all my newly plastered walls and ceilings coming down at the next storm to breach the roofing felt

I retaliated by engaging my trusty old city builder who had to travel forty-odd miles to reach me, and I also engaged a cheap solicitor to respond to the opposition. This he omitted to do in time, and was surprised and mildly apologetic when I received a court summons for nonpayment of debts. The aim of the court hearing was to establish whether the original estimate was too little or too much – and, if one penny too little, the loser (i.e., me) would have to pay up *and* pick up all the costs for both sides. High stakes!

I took a deep breath and went to the most expensive firm of solicitors in the city. I was a little nonplussed to meet my solicitor for the first time. She was young, 5 foot 4 inches tall, pretty, with big blue eyes and curly blonde hair. I soon discovered that she knew her trade well and was as tough as old boots in the most disarmingly feminine way. We attended the preliminary court hearing together, she with her clip-board on which was written her seven-item "wish-list."

The opposition was alone and thirty minutes late, lost, with no clip board, and said nothing after confirming her name. Mine interceded frequently and sweetly: "Sir, would it not be fair to allow my client ...." Each time, the magistrate paused, sighed and conceded, "Well, yes ... I suppose I can allow that." At the end, my solicitor, smiling smugly, said, "Well I got *all* my seven wishes. We're doing fine." Three days and considerable anxiety later, the opposition finally threw in the sponge and withdrew the summons.

It was quite a long time after this that I discovered that my extensive family had been worried sick, thinking I was going to get myself into severe financial difficulties. They were convinced that I was facing bankruptcy and that they would have to bale me out.

The magistrate at the preliminary hearing had ordered the builder to complete the roof slating immediately, so with a very ill grace he rapidly laid on a roofer. The rapidity was sheer malice because my new team were building the porch as fast as they could go. Its roof had to be cut into the house roof front and if the opposition slating was finished before the porch roof ridge went up, the new team would have to cut into and destroy a triangle of new slate

This race gave us the best action/spectator sport I have ever enjoyed. The roofer realised what the urgency was for and did not turn up on the first day "because of snow."

We had none in our bit of Norfolk. On the second day he worked in towards the centre from each side so that about 5 p.m., with dusk falling, he reached the porch roof just as the joiner drove in the last few nails of the ridge truss. Whew! There wasn't quite an audible cheer, but we all downed tools and celebrated with tea and biscuits in the new kitchen.

While the initial building was going on, the only source of electricity, installed by the original electrician, had been a single socket hanging precariously from the meter cupboard. This ran the concrete mixer and all such equipment in use. When visiting, I had to make my way to Oxburgh Hall, a local National Trust 15th Century moated manor house, and buy a sustaining lunch and tea.

6. The rebuilt cottage, with its raised roof and added porch.

Eventually, my cottage was finished, with a raised roof to incorporate an upstairs area, and all the metal-framed "picture" windows being replaced with double-glazed ones matching, as far as was possible, the three remaining Georgian ones. It was underpinned, damp-proofed, re-wired, centrally-heated and all made up to "building regs" standard. I had also had a two-foot-wide *Baxi* fireplace fitted; this is very comforting in windy Norfolk winters, and it takes two-foot-long logs – which greatly reduces wood sawing.

7. Oxburgh Hall, a National Trust 15th Century moated manor house.

3

A Serious Oversight

Sadly, outside all was not well. I had been so delighted to eventually find my place in the country and getting it made habitable that I had not got round to digging a hole to examine the nature of the soil from a gardening point of view. This is the Brecks, an area of fine, wind-blown sand of talcum powder consistency. When one pours water on it silver balls of the stuff rapidly roll down any slight slope to accumulate as a puddle which only reluctantly soaks in over quite a long period, and then disappears, leaving the soil nearly as dry as before. Even after days of torrential rain, any sloping land is only moist down to three millimeters or so.

The little mound on which the cottage stood was the edge of an old sand quarry. The lower level land was the base and a few inches below the surface all was, and still is, pure yellow sand.

8. Breckland, a unique area of sandy heath covered in gorse.

The Brecks, or Breckland, is a unique area of sandy heath covered in gorse and pine extending from north Suffolk to south-west Norfolk. It is easy to dig, even with a deer antler for a tool – hence the name Brecks, because historically it was "broken" and cultivated for a short period and then allowed to revert to its natural herbage which comprises some very rare plants.

I should have known that this was what I had bought because the rabbits excavate great mounds of it on the bank beside my lane. Traditionally, this is rabbit country. It was the Romans who brought them in – damn them (Romans and rabbits). The Normans, particularly those in the monasteries, soon realised that by far the best way to farm the sand was by producing rabbits ("coneys" they called them). Hundreds were contained in warrens covering several acres, secured by vertical turf walls two meters high and topped by gorse. One can still see the traces of these "warren banks" because the land owners who succeeded the monasteries carried on farming rabbits. In mediæval times, rabbit meat was a luxury food reserved for the warren owners. The rabbits were selected for many different coat colours, but the most highly prized was black.

Right up to the late nineteenth century the local industry was rabbit warrening. At the warren centre the custodian lived in the Warren Lodge, a high building with slit-windows from which he took pot-shots at poachers. Pitched battles ensued, reflecting the desperate poverty of folk living on this poor land and who had probably been landless since the Enclosure Acts.

Hundreds of rabbits would be culled daily with the help of nets, ferrets and dogs The meat was sent to feed the cities, and the wool of the underside plucked to make felt for the hat industry – bowlers and toppers – while the rest

9. Mildenhall Warren Lodge dating from 1489 (*left*); and Methwold Warren Lodge and rabbits (painted by Newcombe, 1808) (*right*).

of the pelt was cured for fur. Although the hats were made mainly in Bedfordshire, and the fur-trimmed garments elsewhere, the initial rabbit processing provided a lot of low-paid employment, particularly around Brandon.

10. Warreners on the Elvedon Estate, *ca* 1910.

11. "Out workers" at Brandon in the 1890s, "furrying" – picking fluff off rabbit skins for the felt trade's bowler and top hats.

Nowadays, the standard rabbit control is "lamping," which involves two or three young men in a four-wheel-drive vehicle touring the fields after dark, shooting at panic-stricken rabbits caught in the headlights. This is clearly great sport, but it doesn't happen often, and when I ask them how many they have got the answer is usually in single figures. I acidly point out that the number of rabbits in this area is in triple figures.

The only effective culling control I have involves Steve and Keith with their ferrets and two Harris hawks. The ferrets flush out the rabbits from their burrows, and with the speed of lightning both large female hawks fly off the wrist and impale a rabbit with one claw. The man releases the rabbit, breaks its neck, and then rewards the hawks. Although it may seem gruesome it is a faster death than the other methods. This form of control can be carried out only in the winter or early spring: at any other time the ferret finds a nest full of baby rabbits, which it then eats and falls asleep. Steve or Keith tell me they have lost a ferret, which they may find in a day or two; if they don't, we have a feral ferret (which doesn't bother me too much).

Brandon was also the centre for an even older local industry based on flint. Again, as with rabbits, black was best – Brandon black flint is the *crème de la crème* for working (knapping) and has been a valued commodity for thousands of years. Neolithic flint arrowheads crafted near Brandon at the mines at Grime's Graves have been found as far afield as France and Spain. The extent to which people were trading from East Anglia before the Romans arrived is staggering.

During the Napoleonic wars there was a huge demand for small squares of flint for flintlock guns. It was reckoned that an ordinary flint was good for about twenty-five firings, but that a Brandon black would last through fifty! This difference could have governed life or death on the battle-field at Waterloo. Latterly, flint has been used mainly for building.

The older cottages have a brick framing to their doors, windows and corners, with pure flint, or a mixture of flint and chalk clunch, filling the walls. Norfolk is famous for its huge churches, many with Saxon round towers and built of flint with Barnack stone framing. Some have decorative chequerwork of flint and stone: the flint – usually black – knapped into a regular brick shape. Sadly, many of the knappers died in their twenties and thirties of silicosis. There is still the *Flintknapper* pub on the market place at Brandon.

By the advent of the first world war, the ubiquitous bowler hat of the working-class male Brit was going out of fashion, and land improvement and mechanisation was boosting farming. A limited number of flints for the flintlock guns were still in demand, but the young men went to war and the rabbits were released to the Utopia of freedom and food. The only limit to their fecundity was that when the culling ceased they overgrazed the grass on the poor soil and, since Norfolk is a windy place, the sand once again became windblown. During the "blows" visibility is restricted to a few yards. On one occasion the wind suddenly dropped, dumping its load of sand onto the Little Ouse river, changing its course at Brandon.

Well, back to the present and my potential garden! It is a convexly triangular plot with the lower part bounded by the base of the old sand quarry and the adjacent peaty fields running down to the River Wissey. (The Celtic Iceni tribes living here were known as "The Wissers" so that is what I am!) The longest higher straight side of my garden is at the top of the old sand-pit, bounded by a rare old Breckland permanent pasture covered in rabbit warrens which extend well into my garden. I am constantly risking a broken leg by stepping through the roof of a two-foot-deep rabbit burrow as I go to rescue a flower or shrub which overnight has become covered with nine inches of excavated sand.

Here are moles, too – dozens of them. I rarely find a worm as I dig, and am puzzled by what the moles live on. The general surface of the thin grass is spongy with vole tunnels, and tulip bulbs and crocus corms are listed high on the voles' menu. They must hunt unerringly by smell, so a few days after dibbing in fifty specie crocus corms I find a neat little hole over most of them, and by year three there are none left at all. The nursery recommended these corms for "naturalising," and I suppose one could describe this as a form of "naturalising," but certainly not the one the supplier was meaning.

Is any gardener still reading getting the picture? I could have stuck a pin into a map of England and been luckier than this with my choice of a garden site.

I did not immediately realize the full horror of what I had embarked upon. I brought plants from my town terrace back yard and planted and watered them enthusiastically. They rarely survived longer than a few days: sometimes they were eaten to ground level overnight, and any nursery-bought shrub or sapling was ring-barked.

12. The venerable oak: the biggest, oldest pedunculate oak. Note the newel post for scale.

You may know me well enough by now to realize that that, by itself, would not deter me. I went out and bought 25 meters of one-meter-high chicken-wire and surrounded each plant. Why that high? Ah, what I have forgotten to mention are the roe deer and muntjac who frequent my garden! There are red deer in the neighbourhood, but fortunately they have not found me: if they ever do, I shall need two-meter-high barricades.

I have one very venerable oak on the long boundary, which I suspect is upwards of 500 years old, because it could not grow fast on this soil. I have three other forty-foot-high ones. These are all pedunculate oaks (*Quercus robur*), which is the commonest parkland oak in Britain; amazingly, most have been planted by forgetful jays. My pair of jays are still at it and I transplant their small trees down to my riverside wood – well protected by plastic spirals, of course.

There was room for a couple more oaks along the upper boundary, so in the first winter I bought and planted two well-grown saplings and enfenced them. I planted a Rambling Rector rose at the base of a medium-sized oak, as well as a Kiftsgate rose at the base of a thirty-foot-high spruce, all well manured. As I spent the spring watching them sprout, I happily imagined the high masses of white roses bursting through the canopy and cascading down the two trees in a few years' time.

None of this first planting, apart from a desperately ailing Rambling Rector, survived the summer, despite my strenuous efforts watering each weekend. Now I *was* beginning to get a little depressed.

4

Black Plastic and the Trials of Watering

My mega problem was how to keep the water where the plant could use it. On each TV garden programme I watch, and on nearly every plant I buy, I note that the essential ingredient for successful cultivation is that the soil should be "free draining." I now cringe at any mention of a "suitably well-drained soil."

I have never been really enthusiastic about burying a load of plastic in the garden, but a desperate situation demands desperate measures, and I decided that all my plants, whether herbaceous, shrubs or trees – and definitely roses – must effectively be container-grown. Mind you, the container is big (huge, in the case of trees), but it depends upon my digging a suitable-sized hole, lining it with heavy-duty black plastic, running my fork through it at the bottom for limited drainage and around the sides for the longer roots to escape.

Above ground, most plastic becomes brittle and eventually breaks-up, but buried away from sunlight it seems to last indefinitely. I can then fill it with compost, manure and decent soil (washed off the sugar beet delivered to the nearby Wissington sugar factory). I bought forty tons of the stuff when I planned to make the sunken garden.

With this "container gardening" one good watering will last at least three rainless weeks for a modest-sized shrub. This is important, because the good news is that while the north of England and certainly the south-west is getting unlimited rain, come to sunny Norfolk!

Ten years on we had two-and-a-half months of clear blue, rainless skies, but I am fortunate in having a borehole, without which I could not have made a garden. At first it took me four days, full time, to get round the whole garden watering, and I really needed to repeat-water every two weeks in hot weather. Without the black plastic, all except the more mature trees I had planted – like the red oak and larch – would certainly have been lost. I am hoping that another few years will see more of the trees self-sufficient for moisture.

An automatic irrigation system would be great, but I am container gardening and any water arriving *between* containers is lost. I have begun running black plastic drainpipes from each of six water butts around the cottage and shed to supply water to each plant, but the logistics are formidable. If I do complete this network of drainpipes any heavy rain will be delivered direct to a plant container, and in a real drought I can fill the butts up with a hose. It does mean that the garden will become increasingly dominated by black plastic, though.

I was at Wisley RHS garden the other year, enquiring about a problem I had of repeatedly losing a beech hedge at one particular location (another one is fine). The 20-something-year-old horticulturist offering advice said "Now tell me exactly how you planted this hedge." I told her about the sizable trench I had dug and lined with perforated plastic sheet. She looked horrified and replied that never, *ever* must I put plastic below my plants: they must, but *must*, be free-draining! I bit my tongue before I said something about grandmothers and the sucking of eggs.

Actually there are more advantages of the plastic lining which I had not initially thought of. It tends to keep out moles – not entirely (but more of that anon). It also keeps out honey fungus runners, because, with all the old rotting lilac and plum stumps, much of the ground is badly infected. This is something else I was unaware of when I jubilantly purchased my would-be garden, and it almost certainly accounts for the mysterious death of the young beech hedge.

I shall now risk being a bore and describe how to go about watering an acre of container-grown plants growing in Breckland sand. The essential tools are a spade and a hosepipe linked to a continuous flow of water. The spade is to create a basin round the base of the plant and the hose is to make a moat in it. One then continues to the next two plants and repeats the procedure, returning then to the first plant, by which time the water in the moat has begun to seep into the soil and can be topped up again.

13. Watering a container-grown plant.

This has to be repeated three times in order to complete the watering – providing there are no setbacks, a common one being that the water in the moat disappears almost instantaneously as one stands there hosing. Investigation reveals the water running out some yards further downhill from a rabbit burrow, but more commonly it is a mole-run which has breached the plastic bag, and my best thought is that somewhere a mole is getting very wet. In this case, a round log of wood or a brick is required, and must be stamped firmly into the breach when it is located.

Sometimes the water shows no sign of seeping away at all, and one simply has to remember to return to that plant half an hour later. Of course, when one waters two or three weeks later the procedure must be repeated all over again because the sand, with or without bunny assistance, has gravitated to fill the dried-out moat. Sometimes it is necessary to dig out the tree or shrub which has been buried beneath a foot of sand excavated from a nearby burrow. The line of whitebeams I planted on the bank beside the driveway are particularly vulnerable because the bank is a complex of rabbit warrens. Two of the trees are now protected by vertical paving slabs to deflect the sand. Of course, the ideal solution would have been to enclose the entire acre with meter-high chicken-wire, but this was prohibitively costly and it would still have left the main gate unprotected.

14. Daffodils in February

5

The Fens

Perhaps at this stage I should point out that not all of Norfolk is sandy and drought-stricken. My cottage sits on a little knoll between the extreme limit of the Breckland sand and the peaty land beside the River Wissey where, a quarter of a mile away, the peaty soil is moist. Only a mile away is a tiny remnant of Norfolk fen, preserved as a Site of Scientific Importance: the reed beds covering it used to extend over much of East Cambridgeshire, Norfolk and Lincolnshire.

Ely with its magnificent cathedral is still known as the Isle of Ely because it is built on a substantial hill (at least by Norfolk standards) and before the fens were drained it was the market place for all the fen-caught eels. The cathedral used to be referred to as "the ship of the fens" because it seemed to float above the marshes.

15. Ely cathedral "floating above the fens."

Although the Romans carried out some fen drainage, as did the many local monasteries like the so-called "Fen Five" (Ely, Thorney, Croyland, Ramsey and Peterborough), most draining happened in the sixteen-hundreds at the behest of the Earl of Bedford when it struck him that all the underlying peat would be very fertile and he would get lots more income by growing crops on it. The next thing that struck him was that the people to pay to do this were clearly the Dutch, since they had reclaimed and drained a lot of land in the Netherlands and must know how to do it. This last, in fact, proved to be dubious because they did not seem to know what would happen when one dried out deep peaty fenland.

The Earl's choice fell upon Cornelius Vermuyden, a Dutch engineer who arrived in 1650 to oversee earlier drainage work and continue with it. He brought with him a lot of Dutch engineers to dig ditches and dykes forming drainage channels. There was serious local opposition to this and a lot of sabotage. Many of Vermuyden's engineers were found mysteriously drowned, presumably by "Fen Tigers." We have definitely never had real tigers in our fens, but this was the name given to isolated fen dwellers who made a precarious living fishing and wild-fowling. They were a wild bunch and best left alone – particularly when their livelihood was being drained.

The fens had always provided a refuge for oppressed or solitary people, because they were wild remote places with difficult access. Quite a few early Christian saints and hermits lived in the fens. Later, in the 18th and 19th centuries, the floors of the tiny homesteads were typically made of bricks laid, unmortared, straight on the ground, so that in winter the water rose to the extent that the iron bedsteads might be the only dry spots in the home, but in the spring the water could escape between the bricks.

16. The River Wissey: reeds and rainbows.

17. Fen in autumn.

In my wood there was once a terrace of five cottages close to the river Wissey, where the Ferryman and other families lived; all that now remains is a hawthorn-grown mound, but when my cottage was being renovated I found

18. The ferry cottages at Oxborough: postcard, *ca* 1900–1910.

19, The ferry at Oxborough: postcard, *ca* 1910.

cottage floors laid like this, with two-inch-thick bricks lying straight onto the ground. The first cottage had red brick downstairs and the second buff. With help from my daughter Sophie, who was then living with me, we wheelbarrowed these bricks up to our new cottage where they now grace my sitting room (red) and the adjoining room (buff), but mortared in firmly to meet current regulations. Some of the older cottages in the village still have their original brick floors, and in wet weather the colour of the bricks darkens, then lightens as they dry out. So long as the land is well drained it seems a serviceable arrangement.

The Dutch engineers installed wooden sail-driven wind pumps to move the water towards the sea. Some of these, or their successors, still remain in Wicken Fen, a large area of preserved fenland run by the National Trust.

20. Wind pump for pumping water on Wicken Fen.

After a time the peat dried out, oxidised, rotted and shrank, so that by the end of the 17th century the Welland, Nene and Great Ouse, the huge rivers draining into the Wash, began to flow backwards at each high tide, inundating great tracts of land with brackish water from the sea. Ultimately, the fenland sank by some five feet to become below sea level, and today each of its many rivers and relief channels are flood-protected by high banks – some sixty miles of them. One gets an odd sensation walking along these banks and seeing that the water in the river is markedly higher than the land on each side.

So, in summary, the Earl of Bedford reaped only a limited advantage from his outlay on drainage. Hundreds of poverty-stricken people who depended on the fens for their damp, arthritis-ridden subsistence had to move to the towns. This may have improved their lifestyle but, by the 18th and 19th centuries, many in these Norfolk towns and villages were opium addicts. In fact, Norfolk was notorious in the medical profession for the amount of opium consumed by poor working class folk whose modest pay was barely sufficient for food. I wonder why? Was it poverty-stricken boredom or maybe arthritic pain? Probably not the latter, because it is reported that some children were addicted too.

We do still grow vegetables and sugar beet on the old fenland and we have a local ale called “Fen Tiger.”

21. *Dicentra spectabilis alba*: white bleeding-heart.

6

Within the Pale

The definition of "pale" or "peel" or "pound" is a protective enclosure designed to keep something wanted *in*, or keep a threatening agent *out*. Such enclosures were originally made of wooden palings – hence "palisade" and the Scottish border "Peel tower" or "pele" and the saying "beyond the pale." Historically they were built to protect against marauding mobs of people; thus, the border Peel towers were to keep out the Scottish Reivers (raiders) who used to sing (in a good thick Scottish brogue, I guess) "The Highland sheep are fleeter but the Lowland sheep are fatter; we therefore deemed it 'meater' to carry off the latter."

In the context of my garden, my pale is formed by a two-and-a-half-foot-high double-bar wooden fence, six to ten yards from two sides of the cottage. It is topped up to three feet by a single strand of wire which renders it roe-deer-proof. Four gates which I made access the pale.

To keep out the rabbits, the fence and gates are covered in three-foot-deep chicken-wire, the lower six inches of which is turned out horizontally just beneath the turf on the rabbit side. At the gates there is a strip of chicken-wire buried beneath the threshold. My very useful "hands-on" daughter Sophie built this when she came to live with me for a couple of years just after I bought the land. Her defences have stood the test of time because rabbits run their lives on the simple principle that one moves forwards until one's nose touches a vertical obstruction, and at that point one digs down. Only once has a rabbit Einstein stepped back six inches and then begun to dig there. Fortunately, it decided to think deeply before continuing, and I managed to shove in a brick to stop it quite entering the inner sanctum of the pale. The only rabbit breaches I have had are by baby ones squeezing through a slit in the chicken-wire which I have inadvertently made by running my one-and-a-half horsepower wheeled strimmer too close to the fence. I am a lot more careful now.

22. Penstemons within the protection of the pale.

Many people would advise that the horizontal buried six-inches of chicken-wire must be in quite a deep trench. This is unnecessary. Just below the turf works fine.

Within the pale the land is relatively flat and I grow pretty flowers and small shrubs, and a wisteria grows up the wall around the porch – the scene of the slating *versus* joinery contest – and now spreads 15 feet to either side. At least it *did* – but more of that calamity later.

Initially there were just three ornamental cherries flowering in succession: first *Prunus* "Accolade", with its graceful arching branches and pendulous purple-pink flowers opening in mid-March, followed by *P. shirofugen* and then by *P. shirotae* “Mount Fugi” with its low spreading branches and pendulous clusters of pure white flowers. I have now also planted a cherry grove in a large, plastic-lined bed (for which I resorted to a CAT digger to do the excavating).

23. Wisteria on the front of the porch.

Doing very well beside the wisteria is a beauty-berry, *Callicarpa bodinieri*, and a lovely *Carpenteria californica*. These are relatively tender, but they are south-facing, protected in the angle of house and porch walls and in front by a huge box bush (one of the original ones near the front door).

Recently, when I was pondering the exceptional vigour of the wisteria, I realised that I had never relayed the roof drainage from the base of the nearby gutter fall-pipe to my sheltered plants, because occasionally there must have been sufficient water to flow over the surface and sink into the containers. Fortunately, perhaps owing to the luxuriant growth here, the building regs inspector missed the un-connected fall-pipe.

Within the pale I have improved the soil with many loads of manure and mulch, which allows me to grow just bulbs, dahlias, sedum, rue, hollyhocks, *Hemerocallis*, Michaelmas daisies and phlox without plastic round them, but bit by bit I have had to "contain" many things –

24. The cottage garden: a flint trough, and recycled slate from the old roof: with day-lilies, *Penstemon* and *Scabiosa* (scabious).

like a *Clematis montana* "Elizabeth," *Brunneria* "Jack Frost," primulas, perennial wallflowers and even a mass of different salvias and pentstemons. All of these I had lost in two seasons when planting straight into the soil. Happily it is now a classic cottage garden.

Recently I have realised that the marked deterioration in one key bed could be due to the backdrop of young box I planted five years before. I pondered this and hit on the engineering solution of running an eighteen-inch-deep trench to cut the box roots on that side and at that level, then infiltrating a heavy duty sheet of folded plastic and progressively removing plants, trenching and back-filling across the bed as I unrolled the plastic sheet.

At least pure Breckland sand is normally easy to dig, but when fifty percent of it by volume is densely matted box root and this is found to infiltrate into the bed to a distance of five feet from a three-foot-high hedge, digging

25. Box infiltrating the bed containing *Pulmonaria*, *Sedum*, *Lithospermum*, *Pelargonium*, *Dahlia*, *Astrantia* and purple sage.

26. The box invasion: infiltrating a sheet of heavy-duty plastic.

becomes a great deal more difficult. In fact to my amazement, the infiltration carried on up to the surface, and even tulip and daff bulbs had to be carefully teased free of a mass of box root.

It was surprising anything had managed to flower in that bed. The *Ceratostigma* and *Lithospermum* were doing fine, but they were in the centre of the bed! Having begun, I had to continue for two gruelling days and then manure and replant all the evicted plants on the third.

Now my *Astrantias* "Ruby Wedding" and "Roma" are flowering again, and as prodigiously as they were three years ago – so I guess it was three days well spent. I had obviously been watering the box hedge for the past several years!

The moral of this cautionary tale is don't plant box around beds in a sandy soil, or perhaps consider dedicating the entire garden to box topiary. This will be my default option when I throw in the sponge. Box cuttings root very easily and have the capacity to quickly develop this extensive fibrous root mass. Yew is not so bad. It, too, has fibrous root masses, but they don't seem to extend so far away from the plant. Contrary to what one would expect, rabbits eat yew but they never touch box, so my ultimate default plan will work fine.

27. Within the pale: hollyhock, *Nicotiana sylvestris* and sedum.

In the original land there were two old *Rosa felicita* "Félicité et Perpétué" which had somehow evaded the rabbits. They are fine during their two weeks of annual glory, and very early on I planted some *Rosa complicata* in the pale and these are doing pretty well uncontained. All other roses have to be in lined pits and liberally watered. An early-planted floribunda rose "Iceberg" struggled on, nearly dying each summer until I dug it up and replanted it in a plastic-lined pit, where it is now flourishing. The wider the pit, the happier the plants are, so where possible I plant up to twelve small herbaceous things, or two to three small shrubs, together in an outsized lined pit. The early-planted uncontained Rambling Rector rose under the oak tree was behaving in the same way as the Iceberg, but last year – its twelfth in my garden – it suddenly sprang to life, without help, and is now 15 feet up. In normal conditions it should be approaching the top of the oak tree, particularly as it has the advantage of the roots extending under my heap of manure, but I am grateful for what it can manage. Sadly, three successive *Rosa filipes* "Kiftsgate" have died under the big spruce, and the last two were contained in a large lined pit and liberally watered. This rose has such a reputation for astounding vigour, and each summer I visit its birthplace,

28. Within the pale: honesty, wallflowers, cherry, dogwood and *Spiraea*.

29. The gate in the pale.

Kiftsgate Court in Gloucestershire, and view the original rose occupying a tennis-court-sized area and extending up to the top of three mature beeches! Shall I try again? No; I think I shall give another Rambling Rector the chance to occupy the abandoned pit. After all, it has such an appealingly rakish name.

30. Rambling Rector.

7

The Sunken Garden

Well, I had proved that container growing stuff allowed me to have a garden of sorts, but about ten years ago I was longing to just be able to walk up to a flower bed with a new choice plant, dig a small hole and plant it, and then stand back and watch it thrive.

The lower ground below the bank which marks the side of the old sandpit was occupied by nettles and a bit of rough grass. Nettles do do awfully well here! When I first arrived they occupied every bit of the garden in the summer, apart from an area of rabbit-cropped grass on the higher ground, or where swathes of periwinkle, *Vinca major*, had really got entrenched – bless it!

Rabbits do not eat periwinkle, nettles, evening primrose, ragwort, Italian arum, foxglove, geraniums, green alkanet, snowdrops, daffodils, wood violets, pansies, comfrey, bugloss, box, marrow or potatoes. They eat just about everything else – cultivated and wild – including, staggeringly, yew! I rapidly lost all the yew I planted unprotected, and there were no dead rabbits lying around the stumps. I certainly did not know that box, *Buxus*, was deadly or at least very foul-tasting, though. Another wild plant in the borage family they leave alone glories in the name of Abraham, Isaac and Jacob. It has a pretty spire of blue flowers with reflexed petals that open early in January with the snowdrops.

Well, back to my sunken garden idea. I got out my drawing board – actually a few large, used envelopes – and drew out a rectangle representing the size of a small tennis court, within which I drew a smaller rectangle. With some excavation this would all fit very nicely into the be-nettled base of the old sandpit. I now knew a lot of useful men locally and I hired Mark with his CAT digger for a day and set him to remove the higher side of the sand-pit which was now a sloping bank of sand and nettles. He also excavated a rectangular hole, 12 × 14 feet, roughly in the centre, with the maximum depth of 4 feet but terraced round the sides. This was to be the lily and goldfish pond.

I ordered a large number of concrete blocks – cheap seconds – and set on a modest, Jack-of-all-trades type, Bob the builder, to put walls six blocks deep round the whole area, leaving two gateways. He built attractive, dull red, brick pillars at each corner and on each side of the gateways.

31. Laying the pond-liner in the new sunken garden – with a little help from my friends.

We then laid a tennis-court-sized plastic sheet of the heavy-duty variety used by builders to damp-proof new floors, and lined the entire area, with the plastic rising fifteen inches up the walls on three sides. The width of the plastic fell short by 6 feet on the fourth side, but since this would be mainly gates and paved path it didn't matter. There was a slight slope across the floor so the water would tend to collect at the side opposite the gateways and paved path, so at each corner there I made a one-inch-wide drainage hole in the plastic. The plastic was cut round the pond and then I thought it might be nice to have a concrete block wall round the pond that one could sit on, so Bob, building on top of the plastic, made this one foot high on three sides. The back side was left open for a bog garden. A group of friends were recruited to help lay the black pond-liner. The pond would now be 5 feet at the deepest when filled, and hopefully would trickle over into the bog area.

The bog garden area I double-contained with plastic, making no drainage holes in it at all. I left the soil level with the top of the pond-liner so that the pond would overflow into it. Actually, I have never seen it do this: we never have enough rain to compensate for evaporation from the ponds.

I bought 40 tons of "Wissington" soil. The biggest sugar beet crushing factory in the UK is at nearby Wissington; sourcing the beet from Norfolk and Lincolnshire, they sell an excellent amalgam of soil from the whole area which they wash off the beets, filter and process. It is popular throughout the UK for laying new football pitches. A kindly local farmer delivered a huge trailer-load of sugar beet to the factory and returned to me with the trailer full of soil. I was taken aback by the mountain that 40 tons of soil forms, but most of it made generously deep beds in the sunken garden and some has kept me going for filling "containers." I banked the beds up high on each side of the pond and topped them with massive, interestingly shaped flints.

32. Massive, interestingly-shaped flints.

You remember I said we are in flint country, so I am well placed for a goodly supply of that, living as I do near the millennial-old centre of the flint industry. Close by, there is a handy quarry where I fill my boot with hand-picked chunks after duly driving onto their weighbridge and checking in there afterwards. They usually charge me a fiver, but now I wanted seriously huge flints so I called in to see what they had. They said all the large ones had gone, so I arranged for a carrier to bring me ones as large as he could find. They must have been feeling kindly towards me at the quarry, because the next day they opened up a new bit and the flints that arrived were huge and lovely shapes. Mark's CAT digger was hard pressed to lift the largest into place. There was an anxious moment as he extended the carrying arm forward over the would-be rockery and the back two wheels left the ground. He just released the flint in the right place and all was well.

We could not, of course, complete the wall of the sunken garden until the soil had been stowed as well as the rockery feature flints. Once that was completed I employed a welder to erect six-foot iron poles on top of the walls to support the inevitable chicken-wire at the base, and I hung heavy-duty chain between them to support climbers. The welder also did a brilliant job of hanging and furnishing two matching old wrought-iron gates I had found at a reclamation yard.

33. Welder Merv meditating in the wood by the river at snowdrop time.

I do have to admit that, at this stage, the whole effect was reminiscent of a high-security prison exercise yard, but four years on it has mellowed wonderfully and much of the chain is invisible beneath enveloping clematis, roses, honeysuckle and forsythia.

I planted up the beds, and Bob put attractive coping stones on the foot-high pond wall, with matching paving between the gates. I flirted with the idea of natural Indian sandstone but was warned that this would need constant treatment to stop green slippery algae growing on it. In the end I opted for man-made composite stone, cast to resemble limestone – and very convincing it is. It was as expensive as the sandstone but does not support algae.

34. The well-mellowed sunken garden: a pale pink umbrella plant (*Darmera peltata*) in flower in the middle distance, and pink *Deutzia* and blue *Camassia* beyond.

The paths each side of the pond and between the beds I did with rollered "Carstone" sand and small flints. Carstone is quarried from a seam extending between Hunstanton and Downham Market, and the old buildings nearby are built of small slabs of this with brick frames for the doors, windows and wall corners. This is still being used for prestigious new buildings; when fresh, the stone is quite a bright ginger colour, but it weathers to a dark chocolate brown. The coarse sand is excellent for bedding into a hard, smooth surface which is quite durable. Sadly, it is not weed-resistant, so regular dressings of *Pathclear* are required.

35. A corner of the sunken garden with, left to right, *Rosa* "Mutabilis", *Aruncus*, *Cotinus*, black elder and *Hosta*.

A small corner bed lying outside the plastic lining is dcvotcd to drought-tolcrant plants – a featurc juniper in the corner, aoliums, *Agave* and *Sempervivum* growing between the huge sculptural flints. Initially I popped in some snake's-head lily (*Fritillaria meliagridis*) bulbs just for temporary storage but they do surprisingly well considering that in the wild they are found in riverside water meadows. I can only surmise that the flints retain sufficient soil moisture for early-flowering bulbs. I have left them there. The succulents I have to house for the winter. The sunken garden has fulfilled all my hopes, and looks good throughout spring, summer and autumn.

One of the first plants I bought and installed at the back of the bog garden was another rambling Lady Hillingdon, which does pretty well, but it is constantly reaching up for a high wall so I have to capture the six-foot new shoots and tether them down to the chains. It still flowers prodigiously.

36. *Astilbe* and *Ligularia* in the bog part of the sunken garden.

37. Water lilies in the sunken garden.

38. King-cups by the urn in the sunken garden.

39. The sunken garden with hellebores, *Tulip* "Spring Green," blue *Camassia*, purple hazel and *Clematis alpina*.

40. *Sambucus nigra* (black elder) in flower.

8

Battling with Bunnies – the Ha-ha

The common association with rabbits is the "cuddly bunny." Bunnies always feature prominently on Easter cards and in children's story books. Even I, early morning mug of tea in hand, watching them play tigg from my kitchen window, have to concede that they do *look* jolly as they bounce about, white fluffy tails flashing. Appearances can be deceptive for a gardener. Here is my litany of resentment.

My circular hellebore bed is in the shrubbery which runs parallel to the drive but on the top of a four-foot-high bank. Along the drive, at the bottom of this bank, I have planted a row of whitebeam, *Sorbus aria* "Lutescens," and wild cherry, which I struggle to keep watered despite their containers. The rabbits love burrowing into this bank, and I regularly have to excavate my trees out of a foot or two of ejected sand. Furthermore, the bunnies used to burrow into the shrubbery beneath the perimeter path that tops the bank and then emerge in the hellebore bed, the plants disappearing under barrow-loads of sand. I repeatedly removed this sand and shoved concrete and breeze-blocks firmly into the holes, but the rabbits immediately dug new exits round the obstruction the following night. This continued intermittently for over a year. I had not credited them with such long-term memories and planning abilities or with persistently occupying a particular territory.

I was very interested, as a zoologist, to note that the systemic classification of rabbits is uncertain. I only know this from a 1957 paper written by Alan E. Wood on where rabbits ought to be placed in the phylogenetic tree. He was deeply worried by the evolutionary origin of rabbits.

Were they better related to rodents or to hoofed animals? His paper was titled "What, if anything, is a rabbit?" I am in no doubt that they are certainly *something* – and much more so than I should like.

For the final sorting-out of the hellebore bed, the following winter I dug up every plant, and dug down one-and-a-half feet, throwing the soil to the other side of the bed. I then inserted a thirteen-foot diameter circle of – guess what – heavy duty plastic, folding the spare half up small; and when the semicircular pit was dug, I unfolded the plastic and returned the mountain of soil piled on the other half, to end with my ten-foot-wide bed lined with plastic. The spare 18 inches of plastic I turned up to make a vertical wall around the bed, supported by black plastic netting and sticks, as a rabbit and mole barrier.

41. The plastic barrier against rabbits and moles, under and around the hellebore bed.

Believe it or not, a night or two later, when I had re-planted the hellebores, a rabbit emerged from under the plastic, unable to rise into the bed, and then scratched or bit a hole in the plastic net and sheet from the outside. I think this was just a gesture of defiance, because the rabbit did not gain entry and gave up all further ideas of siting a warren precisely there – but it did make me reinforce the perimeter defences with chicken-wire.

The rabbits have not totally given up even now: their new warren excavation lies right beside the hellebore bed and I regularly fall through the roof of the shallower burrows with serious risk of leg fracture. I should like to know the biological basis of this long-term commitment to a particular spot. It has been this one for twelve years to my knowledge.

42. The new rabbit warren right beside the hellebore bed.

I have employed this labour-intensive method of dealing with drought and box root invasion three times since then: for the small vegetable garden (five days hard work); on the bed by the sitting area surrounded by box hedging (three days hard work); and in the low-walled "dry" gravel garden where I suspected that, since it was beneath a large bay window and up against the house, it would prove too dry to support life (two people, two days hard work).

I have mentioned the various advantages of my plastic-lined pits containing good moist soil: they provide a partial defense against rabbits and moles digging up my plants; keeping honey fungus runners out; and, on one occasion, saving a small tree – the most expensive tree I had ever bought – a *Cercis canadensis* "Forest Pansy."

43. The elegant branches of the *Cercis* "Forest Pansy" arching over the poppies in the wild-flower garden; *Poirus salicifolia* behind.

The elegantly arching branches of the *Cercis* are covered with small pea-style purple flowers in April, and as those begin to go over, the tiny gleaming purple leaf buds unfurl. Throughout the rest of the season it is graced by large heart-shaped dark-purple leaves fluttering on long stalks.

44. *Cercis* "Forest Pansy" in November.

One summer, the leaves began to wilt and it looked worryingly sick. I watered like mad, but to no avail. At that time it occupied the top of a small hill which I have now terraced and surrounded with a "rabbit Ha-ha." An observant grandchild pointed out a hole in the bank a yard-and-a-half below the *Cercis*. We excavated upwards to follow a rabbit burrow leading straight to the tree and discovered that this was suspended in its plastic bag above a void which took three barrow-loads of sand to fill! This was obviously the warren HQ. The following spring, several branches of the *Cercis* had died back but the rest were fine and several years later it is looking stunning again. I would have lost that tree if it had been planted directly into the "soil."

I mentioned the rabbit Ha-ha, which I believe is the only one in existence. The *Cercis* mound was a disaster of water-resistant desertification, with the short grass dead all summer, so I decided I should terrace it. I marked out a smooth semicircle around its base with a length of hosepipe, dug a trench and put in concrete footings. I wanted to build a two-and-a-half-foot-high brick wall matching the new garden-room extension I had just completed on top of the mound – but who could I persuade to build it?

You see, the semicircle "organically" followed the lie of the land, which meant that it was about a foot lower in the middle than at the sides. I knew Bob would be totally recalcitrant to any bricklaying which was not dead horizontal. My welder friend said he knew a bloke with a mass of shoulder-length curly hair and a beard who might take it on. "He looks rather wild but is certainly not," so I must not be alarmed. As if I would be!

So, "Hairy Peter" entered my life and, despite a veritable troll-like appearance, he proved to be the gentlest of people. We got on fine – so well, in fact, that he soon confided in me that our mutual friend had primed him by saying "Whatever she asks, just *do* it – even if it sounds crazy. Take my word – amazingly, it usually turns out OK." And it did! Even Peter conceded that, as long as he viewed the wall from one side, the curvaceous shape was quite beguiling. He didn't use that word, actually, because it is not in the West Norfolk vernacular.

I also installed some ugly metal projections sticking out at the top of the wall on the rabbit side, supporting two

45. The rabbit Ha-ha with poppies. *Cercis* in the background.

strands of wire, just to deter particularly athletic bunnies and deer. I am trying to cover these with miniature-leaved ivy planted by the top of the wall and a minature *Periwinkle minor*. I think I shall have to change to the wild *Periwinkle minor* which will grow out faster. The problem is that when the rabbit Ha-ha was built there was a crescentic void around the base of the hill which I filled with soil washed off carrots – delivered free. The current local business is vegetable arable farming, and as carrots are drenched in fertilizer the soil taken off them grows lush grass which competes with my wild flowers and periwinkle. The fertilizer also runs off the fields and the aquifers that supply our bore-holes are unduly laced with nitrate as well as with calcium from the underlying chalk. I should have paid for some Wissington soil.

Although small as Ha-has go, it has earth right up to the top on the house side, so the wall is not visible from the windows; and on the terrace there grows a riot of wild meadow flowers: dog daisy, meadow chamomile, field marigold, yellow rattle, cornflower, corncockle and several types of poppy. These seed happily on this area so long as I restrict the grass, but none survives outside the wall.

46. Wild flowers on the Ha-ha in June: corn chamomile (white), yellow chamomile, cornflower and corncockle (pink).

One cunning way to restrict grass growth is to encourage the annual yellow rattle, which is a semi-parasite on grass roots. Where there is a good thick patch of it the grass grows to half the height it is elsewhere. The only plants beyond the pale are bugloss, a small geranium and thin rabbit-cropped grass. The *Cercis canadensis* "Forest Pansy" still graces the very top of the terrace close to the large French windows in the wall of the new extension.

9

The Gravel Bed and the Post

To the side of the Ha-ha and immediately below the bay window of the garden room extension I – well Peter, actually – built an eighteen-inch-high wall to enclose an eight-foot by twelve-foot rectangle called "the gravel bed." This is plastic-lined – the hard way – and filled with sandy soil and some manure, covered by black membrane which is permeable to water but not light, and then topped with a four-inch layer of 40 mm diameter gravel. I have slit the membrane to plant a fig, *Ficus carica* "Brown Turkey," beneath the bay window.

47. The gravel bed under construction.

At that spot we buried an old water header-tank, with concrete blocking the holes, to take the fig, which must be contained else it will vigorously inundate the entire gravel bed and more. To begin with, the three leafless stems looked totally innocent of such expansion, but I acted upon experienced advice. Three years later I am pruning it drastically each spring and I find that the white latex which oozes from the cut stems is very irritant on my bare arms. Apparently, being east facing, it may need some protection in the winter, although it has come through several mild ones unprotected. The bay window above must help.

48. The gravel bed in summer, with the newly-planted fig.

I have slit the membrane to plant a lot of small bulbs, crocus, grape hyacinth, miniature daffs and a variety of dwarf tulips. As soon as frost fears subside and the bulb foliage has died back I bring out my large family of *Aoliums* ("Schwartzkoff"), some brown *Sempervivums* and my golden varigated *Agave* which I bought for twenty-five pence ten years ago at a village open garden. It is now two foot across and has pupped!

The ten feet between the new gravel bed and the wall of the sunken garden I desired to be a wide walk of smooth grass with a formal sight-line along its length to a very beautiful "arts and crafts" cast-iron newel post beneath

49. The gravel bed in spring.

the big oak. Together with this I put some beautiful Victorian *fleur-de-lys*-headed cast-iron railings which I had found in a Cumbrian reclamation yard. Originally, so far as my ownership goes, they formed the veranda which graced my city terrace back yard. When the naïve young man who bought my house told me that his builders insisted that the railings were in the way of their scaffolding and asked, "Do you want them?" I dispatched my welder friend and his son to dismantle the railings and bring them back to Norfolk. I had no idea what I should do with them, but I was planning the gravel bed and I hit upon using them around the new bed to support the (yes, you have guessed) chicken-wire.

The problem with the smooth grassy sward idea is that any area that is not cobbled or compacted by vehicles is scuffed up into a number of 4–5-inch-deep rabbit excavations every night, resulting in a mini-Somme battlefield effect and making it impossible to get any continuous grass established. Enter black plastic netting – heavy duty 1.5 cm mesh! I raked the ground level, spread the net and pegged it down with eight-inch lengths of strong wire bent into a hook at the top end. I then chose a wet-weather forecast, sprinkled grass seed and covered with a half-inch of sand. It is essential that each area is completed in one day or it will be hopelessly pock-marked overnight. The grass came through, and although there were some mini rabbit excavations at either end, the netted part remains unscathed.

What the rabbits are digging for totally eludes me. There are no pig-nuts here nor any other sort of edible root. I can only guess it comes from the frustration of basically burrowing animals whose natural inclinations have been devolved to combat myxomatosis. Contrary to my bitter experiences, I am told that rabbits do not now burrow as much as they used to, so I guess this scuffing might be described by an animal behaviour professional as a "displacement activity."

I planted a larch tree in the lower, damper part of the garden, uncontained, soon after I began the garden and it is now nearly 40 feet tall and looks beautiful, particularly as it comes into leaf in the spring and turns golden in the autumn. In April the little bright-pink female flowers appear like miniature pineapples among the short green tufts of baby foliage. They will grow into the green cones which cover the tree in the summer. This tree is fortuitously centred at one end of the ten-foot-wide strip of grass between the wall of the sunken garden and the rabbit Ha-ha and gravel bed. When the larch had been planted none of these features had existed.

Serendipity is the key to my garden design: like Topsy, the garden just grows, one feature begetting the plan for the next. Each plan is conceived in the sleepless period which besets me between 3 and 5 a.m. I had managed to incorporate the *fleur-de-lys* Victorian railings by asking my welder friend to cut them in half and mount top and bottom alternately on the low wall surrounding the gravel bed. Painted grey green they looked great, and I sprayed the fine mesh chicken-wire that they support matt black, which renders it almost invisible. The completion of this, my gesture to formal gardening, was to mount the lovely cast-iron newel post centrally to the grassy walk under the old oak tree at the opposite end to the larch tree.

The base of the newel post is octagonal, so it seemed to demand an octagonal brick plinth beneath it. The paper plan for this plinth took me a long time to draw to scale; with two tiers, each capped with round flint cobbles – larger for the base plinth than for the top one. I showed the plan to Peter who looked distinctly alarmed. I could almost hear him muttering the mantra to himself "Just do whatever she asks. It usually turns out OK." He laid the footings and then procrastinated several months, doing "important" jobs for other people, but eventually submitted to help me.

The whole of the first day was completely taken up in laying the first course of bricks, with repeated measurements made across each of the eight sides to ensure that they were parallel and of the same width. We had just completed this when our mutual friend appeared to check progress. "Well," he said, "Do you know, I thought you were aligning it to the larch tree and not that insignificant little weeping crab!" I stood back and to my horror realised that he was dead right. In our concentration on a parallel-sided regular octagon we had omitted to check that one of the straight facets was facing down the sight-line. It was out by 10 degrees and was facing this wretched little runt crab apple tree.

50. The newel post seen from the gravel bed.

Peter was so devastated I wondered whether he would turn up again the next morning. He did, and before we dismantled the first course of bricks we made a template out of thin plywood, so that the previous day's setting up would not be wasted. The two-tiered plinth was completed without further mishap, and the final capping with round pebble flints gave a very professional finish.

51. The newel post on the grassy walk, with a line-of-sight to the larch tree.

The welder friend mounted the newel post in the centre and I painted it grey-green, but lightened it with silver so that it stood out gleaming beneath the old oak. The brick-work and cobbles were given two coats of water-resistant sealant, keeping them free of algae and looking like new.

I use gravel quite a lot. It is a good weed-suppressant even without an underlying membrane; it stops water running straight off the sand and fixes it down firmly when one hoses. Furthermore, several inches of coarse gravel defeats the voles. My new iris bed is topped by four inches of gravel above a membrane which I slit when I plant. The rhizomes seem to like swelling among the stones and the *Verbena bonariensis* which takes over later in the season loves growing in gravel! It is very "iffy" if one tries growing it in a good bed of soil and rarely seeds there, but I have to weed out a lot of seedlings from the gravel or there would be no room for the irises.

52. Lining the iris bed with plastic. The dew pond can be seen in the background.

10

Ponds and Meres

We have a great many toads looking for breeding ponds in the early spring and I frequently dig them up in rubbly places in the garden in the summer. I initially provided them with lots of old rotting logs to hibernate under, but I have now confirmed what the books say. They prefer hard, man-made rubble – and newts are the same in this respect. I wonder how they managed in grassy landscapes before we started building with bricks and breeze-blocks?

To provide for amphibian shelter I have now used a spare pile of terracotta roof tiles laid out overlapping along the back wall of the sunken garden. The toads spawn in the big pond there and the tadpoles taste too bad for the fish to eat. Because of this they are far more extrovert and sociable than the frog tads. In fact they swarm together, circling the pond in their hundreds.

There are some frogs about, but not many, and their tadpoles are on the menu of the fish and the dragonfly nymphs, so I thought I ought to make a small, round, shallow fish-free pond for breeding frogs.

I read about how to make "dew ponds" (actually in Brazil, but the principle will be the same anywhere). I am sure you have noticed that after a cool night the car is covered in condensation by the morning. The reason is that although the temperature of the soil is well buffered and does not fluctuate much, the air temperature drops at night and anything which is insulated from the ground – e.g., by rubber tyres – will follow the air temperature and attract condensation. This is the same principle that is used to catch drinking water from plastic sheet funnels at night in deserts. Of course, this aroused my interest as a natural way of topping up a shallow pond. I have seen old dew ponds on the Sussex South Downs for the sheep to use. Some say they are very old, maybe mediæval. Like the Brazilian ones they may originally have been laid with straw under paddled clay, but I suspect that the chalk composing the Downs is a pretty good temperature insulator, so maybe only clay was used in their manufacture. In Brazil, straw under the lining clay is recommended, but I guessed empty plastic milk bottles and polystyrene would work. My team of friends set out to collect these useful articles of insulation and we (well, Roger – who knows all that can be known about British pond life) dug a generously deep hole to accommodate them. On top of two feet of plastic insulation I put pond-liner and finished the pond at about 10 inches deep with the top flush to the grass. I do believe it works because after a fair ground-frost there is usually a thin layer of ice on the dewpond but not on the puddles or the large pond.

53. Roger digging the dew pond. (Roger is 6 foot 1 inch tall.)

Having said that, the condensation seems to make a pretty negligible contribution to the rate of evaporation in the summer. I have to top up both ponds during a dry spell. Initially, I used the borehole to fill the new dewpond. Not only is this water very "hard," having reached the aquifer over 100 feet below through three bands of chalk, but it is well laced with nitrate. This part of Norfolk grows a lot of sugar beet, leeks and carrots, all (particularly the last, as I have already noted) requiring high levels of fertilizer which accompanies the rain down to the aquifers.

54. The dew pond.

The first season saw a lot of blanket-weed alga growing in the dew pond (as it also proliferates in the large pond), but during the last season I have only topped up the dew pond from the water butts. Interestingly there has been no sign of blanket weed in the small pond, but plenty in the large one topped up from the borehole. So what they say about fertilizer run-off causing "eutrophication" is perfectly true. A season or two ago I laced the big pond with a blanket-weed inhibitor out of a bottle. It seemed reasonably effective but although guaranteed to be harmless to fish and water weed it had a seriously deleterious effect on the insect life of the pond. I shall not do that again – so I can offer no advice on blanket-weed problems, apart from only using rain water when there is nitrate in the alternative water source.

Barley straw is effective – but *only* barley; wheat or oat straw is no good, and the active principle may be hydrogen peroxide. Several bundles, weighted with stones and sunk in the large pond, did depress the algae for the first summer, but I found out to my cost that it must be removed at the end of the summer else it enters a deleterious stage of rotting which kills the oxygenating weed under the water. All the floating vegetation, like lilies, *Potomagetum*, water hawthorn and even water soldiers seem all right, but leaving the barley straw in indefinitely saw off the sticklebacks, and probably a lot of the insects. Some of the goldfish have survived.

The first spring of the dew pond I put in eight clumps of frogspawn which should have provided more than enough tadpoles for an eight-foot-diameter round pond, but I saw no mature tadpoles at all. They mysteriously disappeared soon after hatching. I know that frog tads do have to make themselves scarce because they are so tasty, but all that was revealed by my careful investigations with a net in the summer was about twelve newts, smooth and crested, fat and sleek and in the pink of condition. Sorry, frogs and dragon flies, but I now have a *newt* pond! In future I shall let nature take its course, "red in tooth and claw." The difficult decision is do I give the newts nourishment next season or not?

55. A four-spotted chaser dragonfly (*Libelulla quadrimaculata*) recently emerged from the lily pond in the sunken garden.

While we are on the subject of ponds, there are some particularly impressive ones in Breckland Norfolk called "meres." They are strange, in that the height of the water does not depend upon the weather but upon the aquifers below the chalk, and varies mysteriously: sometimes the meres are deep and sometimes empty. They are typically circular, and can be anything from a few feet to half-a-mile in diameter. They arose from successive freezing and thawing at the end of the last ice age, a circular lens of ice eventually melting and the overlying topsoil falling in, resulting in a regular depression in the ground. They are known geologically as "pingos" – oddly the word is Inuit for "a mound." They support a unique flora and fauna which can cope with the irregular supply of water.

11

Nearer God's Heart?

"One is nearer God's heart in a garden than anywhere else on earth ..." says the traditional rhyme. Well the Garden of Eden may have been peaceful and lovely, but we fell from Grace, didn't we? Evicted from there, the Garden is now a War Zone. I have already mentioned bitterly the drought, the sand, the rabbits, the moles and the box, but my saga of affliction does not end there. There are the field voles, the shrews, the fieldmice and the rats.

To be honest, I know this range of pernicious rodents only from trapping them in the attic. I am a biologist and kccn country lovcr, and I do not cnjoy having to kill thcsc little furry beasties one bit, but they have inflicted serious damage on my soft-furnishing, bedding, lagging and electric cables. I guess that the most damage inside is done by the mice and rats, but in the winter I trap equal numbers of voles and shrews and even the odd pigmy shrew. I suppose they are just coming in out of the cold – but how does a tiny pigmy shrew, required to eat its own weight in insects nightly, climb up onto the first floor to hide in my cupboards and attic?

In feats of physical endurance the prize must go to the fieldmouse (presumably) which chewed a tennis-ball-sized hole in a plastic sponge mattress and filled it with twenty four peanuts. The mattress was stored in the attic in the roof space and the peanuts were in the greenhouse two doors and a storeroom and a long flight of stairs away – not to mention that the room adjoining the attic is fourteen feet long from the top of the stairs. I reckon that a mouse could only hold a single peanut in its mouth at a time. What a heroic achievement!

Outside, I find only the damage and not the beastie, so I have to guess. I have rabbit barriers round edible plants, and moles eat only worms and insects, so I don't think I can hold either of them responsible for eating my tulips and crocuses. I have planted hundreds of these, and each season only a quarter from the year before come up.

Along the wall of the sunken garden I have a series of stone troughs containing alpines. The tops of the troughs are nearly level with the top of the wall, and the earth outside is also level with this. One year I planted a load of specie crocus in these troughs, and even before the spring I noticed with alarm small neat holes over the surface of the soil – and hardly a single crocus appeared in the spring.

56. One of Sophie's flint troughs.

Small mammals have an excellent sense of smell so there is nothing random about their foraging. A similar fate overtook the early mini-iris bulbs I was given as a present for a talk I gave to the village Garden Club.

Three years ago I had a large order of spring bulbs delivered in the autumn. I sat by the fire and crafted little boxes out of the fine-mesh chicken-wire, sealing three crocus corms of the same colour in each box. Most of these survived the first year and I still have a few clumps of three crocus, but the ones I have dug up are budding baby corms outside the wire baskets so I doubt if they will ever increase in number.

This winter I tried a new ploy. I planted four hundred tulips in beds within the pale and have recently added twenty lily bulbs, at which point I noticed a lot of dug up and mutilated tulips bulbs. I had recently had delivered a huge pile of fresh pig manure to mature for use next year, so I lightly scattered mucky pig straw over all the planted beds. The whole of the pale now reeks dreadfully but, considering how good these rodents' sense of smell is, I hope it will keep them at bay a lot longer than it will me.

This winter I have a small beastie in my greenhouse. Because something was eating most of the beans I plant in the vegetable garden, a few days ago I planted forty broad beans in individual containers to bring on and plant out later. Today I found the tell-tale holes and no beans at all. I intend to find out who my guest is, so I shall get a catch-them-alive trap.

My vegetable garden is small, so I only attempt to grow the things I enjoy eating. Mainly, this amounts to beans, mange-tout peas and asparagus. Oddly, the asparagus does not need protection, but the rest do. I have to plant the peas and beans two or three times to achieve a whole row. For the last couple of years I have harvested no strawberries – even the flowers were eaten – and I eventually, by dint of putting a glass enclosure round them, got a promising row of broad beans (my favourite). When they were ready for harvesting I found the pods still in place, but bearing bean-sized holes all along and *no* beans! *Voles!*

In the past I have also suffered a great deal of garden damage from much larger furry beasties – cattle. You may remember that I have bovine neighbours in the field at the top of the old sandpit. Early in my rural occupation, before the garden was established, we woke up one Sunday morning to find small groups of cows and young bulls gazing in at us with interest through each window. They had paced daintily, in line-astern formation, along the shallow trenches marking out the newly planned slate path for the pale.

57. My bovine neighbours.

One New Year's eve much later, I and a couple of my friends were setting off some seasonable fireworks when we heard munching. Rabbits? They can't be *that* big, my friends said – and there, under the big spruce, eating ivy, were the cattle from the field above the sunken garden. The battery for their electric fence had gone down. We returned them to the field, but next morning they tobogganed down the steep sandy bank from their field, trashing a young eight-foot-high black pine, and tore through a lot of rabbit defenses to eat the ivy high in the hedges. Eating the ivy didn't matter too much, but they ripped up the black plastic netting along the hedge protecting a line of young *Pyrocantha* bushes. It took four days to repair. After a prolonged campaign I have now managed to get that herd properly fenced in, but there is another nearby and I now have a substantial metal swing-bar which can close the gateway when I am away.

Well that is enough griping about the furry inhabitants of my fallen paradise. Let's start on the plants – *weeds* in fact – and the fungi.

In the beginning, my rural life was dominated by nettles. I have mentioned that I also own one-and-a-half acres of wood by the side of the river Wissey, a quarter of a mile from the cottage, and that there is a long mound there representing the foundations of a terrace of four tiny cottages which housed the ferryman and some other families. I have found in the surrounding jungle some brickwork which must be part of a wall of their WCs built at an odoriferous remove from the cottages. There are some venerable apple trees, too, one said to be "Warner King," and where the cottage gardens would have been there was a sea of six-foot-high (I am not exaggerating) nettles. The ground is beautiful rich moist peat. If only I had it in my garden! The ferry stopped running in the early 1920s, and the cottage inhabitants were moved out soon after World War II.

When I arrived on the scene there was about half an acre of nettles covering the open area and more in the wood, which was composed exclusively of brittle willow some sixty feet tall, wild plum, ground elder, snowdrops and winter aconites. The flowers are a joy in the spring and well adapted to life there because their foliage disappears as the nettles begin to grow.

After a season of nettle killing experiments I found that a mere four to five months under any light-opaque cover totally did for them. I begged a multitude of old carpets and bought a lot of black heavy-duty polythene for this job. I have to confess that aesthetically the nettles may have been preferable.

After five months I laboriously skimmed off the top three inches of soil and nettle compost and barrowed it up to the cottage; up, of course, from river level to the sandy mount where my cottage sits. The benefit to my cottage garden seemed minimal and it had a negligible effect in reducing fertility in the wood area but it was tremendous exercise.

I planned to make a wild flower meadow in the wood, and one does need impoverished soil for that. I seeded the cleared area with grass and wild flower seed and bulbs including bluebells, looking forward to a lovely meadow in the following years.

There are not so many rabbits down there, but deer enough to eat all the dog daisies, the young bluebells, the wild garlic, the cow-parsley and even the knap-weed. The only thing I have won is the wild geraniums. I guess they are bitter or poisonous, but sadly they do not spread. A few forget-me-nots struggle through most years.

My “Waterloo” came when I had cleared such an area that I could not cut it often enough to keep out the nettle seedlings which pour in from the wooded bit. Two years would have seen it revert to the state I found it on arrival. My final response was to give the whole area to a friend in return for his mowing it three or four times a year. At least I have not yet had to watch five years blood and sweat totally wasted.

The trees I planted in the wood are more of a success story. I now have two groves of 25-foot-high alder, three 30-foot ash trees, some tall silver birches, a larch, two beeches, a balsam poplar (a cutting I took 18 years ago – 40 feet tall now) and several new apple trees. The last only fruit once in a while, probably because the wood is a trap for cold frosty air rolling down towards the river. Most of the larger trees are now 30 feet high with nine-inch-diameter trunks. They certainly outstrip the trees I have planted around the cottage. To begin with, all these young trees had to be carefully deer- and rabbit-protected, but they are well toughened off now.

Well, finally, back to the garden. I have proved that container growing allows me to have a garden of sorts on Breckland sand, but some of the small shrubs and trees do tend to become "bonsaied." This is particularly true of the ornamental crab apples, the whitebeam and the weeping pear. They flower and fruit, but their overall size has hardly changed in seven or eight years. This winter I plan to drive biggish stakes through the polythene lining and fertilize and manure well. They may be pot-bound, and I hope their roots are sufficiently well grown now to cope with a bit of drought.

Heigh-ho! There is, of course, the default plan – just box topiary everywhere!

Rudyard Kipling's take on it is:

Our England is a garden
And such gardens are not made
By singing "Oh how beautiful,"
And sitting in the shade.

12

Pets and Other Things

Perhaps you have been wondering whether I share my garden with any friendly, supportive beings. So far, this amounts to the handful of people who help me and who are certainly both.

I do not have pets, because I travel away a lot and my freedom is important, but it is reassuring to have someone around when I return home and, oddly, I do get a strange feeling of support from PP – Pet Pigeon. She is a wood pigeon, one of many in the vicinity, but she first came to my notice nearly five years ago when I watched, fascinated, as she jumped into the new dew pond, flapped mightily, steering herself to the middle and back, then climbing out and shaking herself. Not content with this odd behaviour she promptly bent over, dived in and repeated the performance. After this I just wondered whether it was all an accident as she tried to get a drink, so I put two large flints at the edge of the pond and haven't seen her do it again. Perhaps she just decided that swimming was not a pastime she really enjoyed.

I can distinguish PP from a multitude of relatives because her sear is small, making her orange beak slightly longer and more hooked – giving her a rather disdainful appearance as she views me with guarded suspicion. Her favourite perch is the gate to the pale in front of my kitchen and sitting room windows. She spends most of her time there, keeping a watchful eye on her territory beneath the bird feeders, and any invading pigeon she sees off aggressively. Very often, as she crouches with ruffled feathers and her head sunk in her chest, I wonder what she is thinking about: just dozing, perhaps. Even patrolling her territory she moves about ponderously, as if planning what to do next. Her relatives are always much more alert and busy.

When I return from a couple of weeks away it is always with a feeling of relief that I see PP perched on the gate. After all, pigeons are a popular food for peregrine falcons, and she does present a sitting target. It is strange how little a solitary human like me demands from a pet.

58. PP and partner on their gate.

After two years or so I discovered her sex when she acquired an admirer – PPP (I shall leave you to work that out). She actually allows him to share her gate, although he seems to regard it as an inappropriate place to do his courting, so he calls only briefly. Wood pigeon courtship is quite touching. He bows deeply, fanning out his tail, then they preen themselves and kiss. Yes, they lock beaks and rock to and fro for several seconds and if, after another quick preen, she crouches down, he mounts her. The first time I voyeuristically watched this from my window I expected PP would disappear to arrange the six or so crossed twigs which serve wood pigeons as a nest and then have to lay and incubate a couple of eggs, but this has never happened and she has remained squabless.

One evening I heard a noise, as if large cardboard boxes were being thrown up to the ceiling. I traced this to the new bathroom off the greenhouse where I store the bird food, and there was PP trapped behind the glass shower guard in the bath. When I looked in, she stopped flying up and down and perched on the top of the guard. I bent down and approached gently cooing "PP" repetitively, which she used to tolerate in the garden. As I got up to her she surprised me by jumping onto my head; so, cooing about turning round, I shuffled to the door where she took off to freedom. She is always trying to get into this bathroom to tidy up birdseed that has escaped from the bins, so I have to make sure that the door is shut – but she got in once again, perched on the shower guard but failed to jump on my head, so impatiently I slid my hand up behind the guard and caught her by both ankles. She went berserk, and although I rapidly fastened her wings and launched her out of the greenhouse door, she has viewed me with deep suspicion ever since. That was three years ago, and still I am not allowed to walk close to her in the garden cooing "PP."

So much for my unsupportive pet, but she is a very unusual wood pigeon. The most damage she ever did was when she brought PPP into the greenhouse and found the bathroom door closed but the house door open. I was alerted by the noise of violently breaking glass and rushed in to find them both doing vertical take-offs on the window sill in an effort to fly through closed double-glazed windows. I had all the medicine bottles and others I had dug up in the garden and a sweet little china mouse on this sill. They were shattered all over the floor.

Interestingly, wood pigeons have such powerful pectoral muscles that they are one of the few birds that can take off vertically. I guess this is why they are rarely run over on the road – well, that and their IQ which is relatively high. Our Norfolk roads are always liberally sprinkled with squashed pheasants, presumably because they are not so athletic and are exceptionally stupid. The cock birds in full plumage are spectacularly beautiful, but decision making is not their forte. As cars approach they will stand in the middle of the road turning their heads back and forth trying to decide which way to go, until they end up as a tasty meal for the crows. I think they are "turned on" by the colour red, because the cock birds have well-developed red wattles and do fight. I have a red car and often, as I drive in, the resident cock challenges my car to a fight by stamping aggressively and bobbing up and down from a crouching position. That really *is* stupid. There is always one cock patrolling the garden, but not the same bird for long – presumably because of the gunfire which is a feature of Saturdays here.

Pheasants, of course, are not indigenous and hail from Asia, but they are bred here for shooting. Winter food like maize is grown for them and gamekeepers assiduously shoot magpies and foxes – "vermin," they term them. I am bitter about this, since I do not approve of killing things just for sport, and the magpies and foxes are part of our wild ecology. If there are no foxes the rabbit population escalates – but then even *they* are not native to Britain. This may sound a bit zoologically purist, but that is the way I feel.

Well, so much for my unrewarding pets, but way back in Chapter 5, I promised to fill you in with the more recent history of the wisteria. You remember it had grown to cover the porch and extend fifteen feet along the side walls. It no longer does this because an outbreak of honey fungus took out twenty-odd feet of my sheltering perimeter lilac hedge to the south of the cottage opposite the south-facing porch. The following winter we had continuous gale-force southerly winds sweeping up from the river, and the wisteria covering the front of the porch and reaching round the right hand side, died. Fortunately, it was planted just round the left-hand porch corner, close to the sheltered bed behind the big box, so it is fighting its way back.

My diagnosis was confirmed when a mass of honey fungus toadstools appeared at the base of one of the dead lilac trees in the hedge. After photographing them I barrowed stump and fungi down towards the wood and tipped them in a drainage ditch well away from any trees. I mechanically excavated a large bed which had been cleared by the honey fungus infestation, removing all trace of the dead lilac, and I plastic-lined it.

The next summer I visited the Bishop of Norwich's open garden on the National Garden Scheme, where I found enormous evergreen bamboos growing. One variety had old twenty-five-foot stems five inches in diameter – the sort that are used for scaffolding in places where they grow. I coaxed one of these from the Bish's Head Gardener. I did pay him for it, but I was a bit disconcerted that he had such confidence in his knowledge of the six or so different species of bamboo in the garden that he hadn't even labeled them in his nursery. I reckon he *did* give me the right one because three years on it has formed a substantial evergreen clump fifteen feet high. This could, of course, replace my garden default option of box topiary by giant bamboo everywhere, but for the moment it promises to replace my shelter belt and protect the wisteria. I reckon bamboos like moisture so I think escape outside the lined bed would not be to its liking.

59. Honey fungus on dead lilac in the south shelter belt.

Before I start talking about plants again I must mention some more birds – in particular, the geese. I can think of no more emotive cry of the wilderness than the mewing of geese as they fly to their evening roosts on water. In the autumn there are scanes of migrating geese flying over, keeping in constant calling contact, to spend the winter on Norfolk lakes. Some have come from Siberia and some from beyond the Arctic circle.

Throughout the year there are buzzards circling high on thermals above the Brecks, like huge wide-winged moths. In the summer, barn owls hunt to feed their families: they hunt mainly by sound, so they patrol back and forth, swooping up and down, seven to ten feet above the grass.

The little birds keep me constantly amused, because I have feeders in front of the windows of my kitchen and my bedroom. I feed five different species of tit – blue, great, coal and long-tailed, and my favourite neat little marsh tit.

I sincerely hope we marauding humans can find a balance to keep viable what wild nature we still have.

60. Bishop of Norwich's bamboo in the usual southerly gale.

13

These are a Few of my Favourite Trees

William (Willa) Cather (1876-1947) wrote: “I like trees because they seem more resigned to the way they have to live than other things do.” They can live for so long, too. I sometimes ponder what it must feel like to be a tree: to feel one’s roots slowly pushing into the soil, one’s sap rising, and young leaves beginning to unfurl and move gently in the spring breeze.

Maybe you remember my initial policy of planting trees and shrubs quickly so they had the maximum time to grow into mature beauty and provide shelter for the garden. Now, nearly twenty years on, my initial plantings are looking good. The only problem is the *wind* – to which Norfolk is prone with a vengeance. Sometimes it blows continuously hard for days, usually from the south west.

The red oak is 25 feet high and, fortunately, straight. Many of the other trees are tending towards the “coastal” and need heaving upright with post and cord.

Another tall tree, actually probably 40 feet now, is the larch, which had to be jacked upright for a couple of years because it threatened to actually keel over. Sand is not a firm base. The tree is fine and pretty straight now; fortunately, such a small list to counter-windward as it has, is in line with the axis of my formal grass avenue between the larch and the newel post pillar, so it doesn’t disturb the purity of my formal sight-line. The tree looks great as it comes into leaf, covered with the tiny pink cone-shaped flowers preceding the real cones. It looks superb in November as it blazes into a spire of yellow-gold, and an early frosty night renders it ravishingly beautiful (see font cover).

Another tree which also metamorphoses through the seasons is the *Cercis* "Forest Pansy." This, at twenty-five pounds sterling, was – as I mentioned earlier in Chapter 8 – the most expensive sapling I had ever bought (I have matched this once or twice since). It is deciduous, but in early spring the arching dark branches are covered with tiny purple pea-flowers, quickly joined by gleaming purple leaflets. These may lose their gleam later, but they retain the intense purple and become large and heart-shaped, constantly fluttering on long stems. In the autumn the leaves change bit-by-bit into gold and rich terracotta. It is an amazing sight to see these back-lit by the November sunshine. You may perhaps remember the harrowing incident when the rabbits established a cavernous hall for their warren immediately underneath this tree; fortunately, now that it is in the protection of the wild flower extension bounded by the rabbit Ha-ha, the tree is safe and flourishing at about ten foot high.

A favourite, bought soon after I arrived in Norfolk, is the deciduous *Cornus* "Eddie's White Wonder." Now about eight foot tall and similarly broad, with spectacular dark-centered white flowers three inches across in spring, it turns a gorgeous mixture of gold and orange in November.

A tree that looks splendid in March is the dogwood *Cornus mas*, also known as Cornelian cherry from the edible small red fruits it bears in September. The flower buds begin to sprout as bright yellow pom-poms in February, and the tree soon looks like a gigantic canary. Mine has golden green leaves throughout the summer.

Another attractive tree is the *Cercidiphyllum japonicum* which has delightful rosy leaf shoots early in the spring and goes a yellow-gold in autumn or brilliant orange in some years. The fallen leaves smell strongly of caramel. This tree usually prefers a damp place but holds its own here, just dropping some yellow leaves during a hot summer. This year it lost every leaf in August so I desperately cut down one of its three trunks. It bravely grew a new set of leaves even larger than usual.

61. *Cornus* "Eddie's White Wonder" in flower in April.

62. *Cercidiphyllum* in autumn with *Cotinus* "Grace" behind and *Cornus mas* beside it.

63. *Cornus mas* in February.

64. Crab apple "Red Sentinel.".

A list of my favourite trees would not be complete without a mention of the crab apples. They are wonderful value, being covered with blossom in the spring and, come October, apples. I have tried several varieties: the yellow ones rot at the first frost, the orange ones are not much better, but Red Sentinel is superb. A gracefully drooping tree, it bears an abundance of bright red fruits which are not eaten by birds, do not succumb to frost, and hang on the tree until early March in a mild winter. It would be a pity to pick them to make apple jelly, but a small handful added to wild crab apples gives a lovely ruby jelly.

Another favourite of mine is *Cotinus*, the "smoke bush." I have the smaller-leaved *Cotinus coggygria* "Royal Purple" which looks lovely all summer and has good autumn colour; my out-and-out favourite, however, is the larger much more vigorous "Grace" with its four-foot-long erect branches bearing large, deep purple-red leaves which turn in the autumn through gold to red. I am writing this nearing the end of November and there are still bright red leaves waving at the tips of the branches. I have three of these beauties which reach a height of at least ten foot in the sand, but they may be over-vigorous for smaller, more fertile gardens. The smoke bush gets its name from the delightful hazy cream or pink flowers which feather the bushes in June: the old inflorescences are misty with dew each morning in the autumn.

Since I have extended my terms of reference to shrubs, I must mention the evergreen *Carpenteria californica*. As its name implies, it needs a protected site here. I grow it in the angle of the porch and house, shielded from the southerly gales by one of the garden's original huge box bushes. For the first few years it was a joy in the summer, covered by masses of gleaming white three-inch-wide flowers, each bearing a tuft of bright yellow stamens. The waxy dark-green leaves show them off to perfection. Last year was dry, and its lined pit did not supply enough water, so it nearly died and lost all the leaves from the trunk and lower branches. I dug up all the smaller plants in that bed, and the following week totally lined the bed with each individual pit-liner flattened out and pasted close to the new lining plastic. I had successfully achieved this before in other beds, but did I dare prune back the *Carpenteria*, or would that be the kiss of death? I decided to try. Result: the kiss of death! I have bought a new one.

Another incumbent of this bed, which survived last year's drought reasonably well but is looking a bit leggy, is the beauty berry *Callicarpa bodinieri* (probably "Giraldii"). This has groups of bright violet flowers in the spring, succeeded by bunches of tiny lilac berries which survive on the bush well into the winter. In the United States I have seen what is surely a variety of *Callicarpa* with elegant arching branches bearing the tiny lilac flowers and berries uniformly to the branch tips. It also comes in a golden foliage variety. Being unable to find this on my return to the UK, I acquired some cuttings on my next transatlantic visit, and these have rooted well. We shall see what happens next spring.

Thereby hangs a tale. An American friend kindly gave me these cuttings sealed and labeled in a strong plastic bag and three other labeled bags each containing unusual irises. I put them into the middle of my hold luggage "wheely" bag, surrounded by clothes, suspecting that they might be picked up as suspicious drugs by the scanner at the airport. We landed at Heathrow and I reclaimed my bag thankful that there seemed to be no message that I should be detained at customs, so I carried on through the green door. When I opened my bag at home there were the four bags lying right on top of all my clothes, with a printed slip from customs apologising for any damage that might have occurred opening my bag when it “happened” to be selected for a spot check! I am fairly sure I should not have been importing plants, so I reckon that that customs officer must have been a gardener.

65. *Carpenteria californica.*

14

Norfolk Plant People

Alan Bloom was a horticultural legend. He died in 2005 aged 98. Alan bred or named 170 plants, wrote 27 books, opened a steam museum and created an extraordinary garden and nursery at Bressingham, Norfolk. His son Adrian now runs it. His family were thought to have been Huguenots who had come to East Anglia with Cornelius Vermuyden, the man who drained the fens in Charles I's reign. If this is so, they were clearly not amongst the many Dutch engineers who were found mysteriously drowned in fen dykes, presumably by "Fen Tigers."

As a boy, Alan earned quite a bit of pocket money planting seeds and pricking out young plants to sell to locals. He was nothing short on enterprise, and at fifteen he left school with a passion for plants, inherited from his father who was an innovative market-gardener. His first job was in a nursery in Wisbech, Cambridgeshire, but he soon grew tired of being told what to do for 15 shillings a week, and joined his father's business.

By the age of 24, he had started his own nursery in Oakington, Cambridgeshire, having invested his £10 savings in alpines, which were then beginning to gain in popularity. He built up a wholesale business, and bred new varieties of aubrietia, pinks and – a special favourite – campanulas. The 1930s was a time of expansion in the trade, with a new class of people able to buy a home with a garden, and by the outbreak of the Second World War, Blooms' Nurseries had become one of the largest of its kind in England.

Alan spent most of his long life at Bressingham Hall in Norfolk. He bought the house and 200 acres which were to become the famous nursery, Blooms of Bressingham, in 1946. It was there that, in the 1950s, he invented a new style of gardening, using herbaceous perennials in island beds, in his six-acre Dell Garden. He also worked as co-founder and first chairman of the Hardy Plant Society.

There was always a strong commercial idea behind Alan's enthusiasms. He had a passionate desire to introduce the gardening public to herbaceous perennials: these were the plants that he was busy breeding, but they were generally seen only in the borders of grand houses where there were a couple or more gardeners. Some of the plants he raised, such as *Achillea* "Moonshine" and *Agapanthus* "Bressingham Blue," are still favourites with discerning gardeners. Alan saw island beds as a way of promoting a wider interest in these plants, and of encouraging people with smaller gardens to be more adventurous with perennials. In no time, island beds sprang up in gardens all over Britain. The principle was to remove a round or oval space in the lawn – the size would be determined by the size of your lawn – and then plant taller perennials in the middle, grading out to small bedding plants round the edge. Effectively, this was a double herbaceous border, but you could walk all round it and you didn't need a fence or wall.

Not too far away, at Attleborough, we have Peter Beales. Located in the heart of Norfolk, his beautiful 3-acre gardens supply all classic roses by mail order or direct from the garden, as well as a wealth of rose knowledge. Peter is a renowned RHS Chelsea Flower Show gold medalist and often displays the centre-piece roses from his winning exhibits. You can soon lose yourself in the tranquil, rose-filled surroundings.

Another person who deserves a mention is Dr Sidney Long, the founder of the very first UK naturalist trust, now known as the Norfolk Wildlife Trust, an organization which encourages volunteers to protect and study our unique natural habitats. A commemorative plaque to him is to be found beside Langmere, one of our largest meres.

Of course, we also have a royal garden at Sandringham, where traditionally the Royal family spends Easter; this is open to the public, together with the large wooded estate surrounding it.

66. *Prunus kursar* blossoming in February.

15

Gardening Philosophy

An old Chinese proverb says: "If you want to be happy for a day, get drunk. If you want to be happy for a week, kill a pig. If you want to be happy for a month, get a wife. If you want to be happy all your life, plant a garden." A trifle chauvinistic, perhaps, but – with the provisos I have mentioned in the preceding fourteen chapters – the last bit of advice may have some truth. And since the subject of gender has been raised here are my observations and deductions.

"Hands-on" gardening seems to be a largely feminine pursuit. Look in the pages of the *Yellow Book of Gardens Open for Charity* in the National Garden Scheme and you will notice the predominance of women gardeners over men, and this is emphasised when one visits the gardens. The *Yellow Book* may record, in a rather dated fashion, that the garden belongs to Mr and Mrs John Smith, but it is almost always Mrs Smith who shows you round and John who modestly claims that he merely mows the grass and builds little walls where he is told to.

Women are usually in evidence in mediæval manuscript gardens, too. Admittedly, they are often weeding for a pittance – threepence a day in 1500 – but just sometimes they are directing operations.

The early convents and abbeys, such as the Abbess Hilda's (614–680) in Whitby, served the local community's medicine needs. Very often the cloister would have served as a walled herb garden. It was not only the ecclesiastical women who gardened. Thomas Tusser wrote in 1577:

In March and April from morn to night,
In sowing and setting, good housewives delight.

67. Women weeding and working with men in the garden.
Detail from *Spring* by Jacob Grimmer, 16th Century.

Another aspect of the study of plants which is traditionally gender-stereotyped is witchcraft – which tends to merge with herbalism and pharmacy. The appalling records of seventeenth century witch hunting makes it plain that an intelligent woman with a sound knowledge of plant law would have been wise to keep it under her hat – and make sure that *that* was not black, tall and pointed, of course!

In bygone years it was surely the women who did the gathering as opposed to the male pursuit of hunting, and meat was probably just an occasional feast treat. It was the roots and berries which really kept body and soul together most of the time. Although we shall never know for certain, it is a fair guess that the earliest farmers were

68. A lady supervising her woman gardener.
Illustration from *Cité des Dames* by Christine de Pisan, *ca* 1475.

the womenfolk. The men were making grand designs for temple building and working out how to shift enormous Sarsen stones considerable distances. From a theoretical standpoint, too, it is likely that it would be the gatherers of roots, seeds and berries who would have come up with a more efficient way to feed the community.

Archaeological evidence is now suggesting that the first crop and animal cultivation occurred in many different parts of the world as early as 12,000 years ago. It seems that this was often on a small scale – "gardening," in fact – alongside the old hunting-gathering traditions.

My thesis is borne out by the membership of the local garden and allotment societies: predominantly female. There is an exception to this in the vegetable area. Quite often there are enthusiastic men working there. I was highly amused by a rueful story told to me by a very keen gardening male friend. He had an allotment quite close to the centre of Leeds where he grew flowers, but he found that he was being ostracized by the usually companionable male vegetable gardeners. It eventually dawned on him that it was pure sexism. The over-riding association of a man growing flowers to the West Yorkshire fraternity was that he must be "gay." This is quite an old story, so I hope it will no longer hold true.

It does seem that women, by and large, enjoy nurturing, whether it be small children or plants. There is such satisfaction in planting a seed and seeing it germinate and grow into its preordained shape and habit. To be truthful, it is likely to create far less work than a child would, too.

As Flanders and Swann somewhat cynically put it in "Misalliance":

Poor little sucker, how will it learn
When it is climbing, which way to turn?
Right? Left? What a disgrace!
Or it may go straight up and fall flat on its face!'
Said the right-hand thread Honeysuckle
To the left-hand thread Bindweed:
"It seems that against us
All fate has combined ...
Oh my darling, oh my darling
Oh my darling Columbine,"
Together they found them the very next day.
They had pulled up their roots and just shriveled away,
Deprived of that freedom for which we must fight –
To veer to the left or to veer to the right!

Leaving politics aside, isn't that an amazing message all encapsulated in a tiny seed? Not only in which direction to spiral, but the precise angle at which the leaves and branches will spring from the main stem, their size, colour and seasonal responses. Plants are overwhelmingly clever and so self-sufficient! All they ask are sunlight, water and a modicum of nutrients. That doyenne of English gardening, Gertrude Jekyll (1843–1932), wrote that: "In gardening one has not only to acquire the knowledge of what to do but also ... what is well to let alone". Yes, leave it to the plants whenever one can!

I have described how I have managed to make a creditable garden out of very unpromising material, and I have confessed that many of my trees and shrubs are somewhat "bonsaied" – but there is yet another Chinese proverb which says: "The best time to plant a tree was twenty years ago. The second best time is *today.*" I did plant trees some eighteen to twenty years ago and they should be reaching for the sky by now, but at least they *are* alive.

Struggling as I do to coax my plants to grow, often with insufficient water, I am rewarded by the least expected flourish of leaf or flower. I regularly hear myself saying with feeling, as I walk around my garden, "Well done, that plant!" I guess this is a triumph I should be denied under really good gardening conditions.

So time passes, and I carry on eternally planning the next garden project – which I know is mistaken. "Cueillez des aujourd'huy les roses de la vie" (Pierre de Ronsard, 1524-1585); and here I am, with my eyes fixed on the horizon of next season, and no time to just sit and look at my garden. Well, anyway, here's hoping for a few more years' gardening yet; and I shall finish with a similar sentiment in a poem by Robert Herrick (1591-1674):

Gather ye rose-buds while ye may,
Old Time is still a-flying.
And this same flower that smiles today,
To-morrow will be dying.